Community Engagement
From Concept 2 Implementation

8 Steps to Unlocking Your Creative Ideas

CATHERINE E. TROTTER

ISBN-13: **978-1500135843**
ISBN-10: **1500135844**
Printed in the United States
North Charleston, South Carolina

Community Engagement
From Concept 2 Implementation

8 Steps to Unlocking Your Creative Ideas

TABLE OF CONTENTS

DEDICATION

This book is dedicated to Founders, CEO's, Executive Directors and Community Leaders that manage philanthropic organizations and facilitate community engagement projects.

Your leadership is what continues to pave the trail and open up opportunities that will allow our communities to flourish. The systems that you have built are the building blocks for the future of a healthy community.

…unlocking your creative ideas begins
TODAY!

<u>INTRODUCTION</u>

Community Engagement from Concept to Implementation will reveal eight steps to unlocking your creative ideas around the development, organization and execution of a systemic approach to building community engagement projects. The book will define the concept of "community engagement" and will peel back the layers on how to become an effective leader in "community organizing".

The reader will discover "how to take ideas and turn them into a cohesive strategic plan that can be executed". Each step will teach readers how to examine their assets, how to develop a strategic alliance, how to create a time line, how to develop a team, how to execute on the plan and create a ripple effect that will yield results ten years out from the start of the project.

Community organizing is all about building grassroots support. It's about identifying the people around you with whom you can create a common, passionate cause. And it's about ignoring the conventional wisdom of company politics and instead playing the game by very different rules.

~Tom Peters

Vision → strategic plan
Strategic plan → goals, objectives
                          ↓
                    premeditated desired
                      outcome
Why community engagement?
   fill a void, a need
                  (.Gila)

<u>STEP 1</u>

WRITE THE PLAN

STEP 1
Write the Plan

Step 1: Write the plan

In order to be effective and to have a sustainable organization, one must have a clearly defined strategic plan that directs the organization growth decade to decade. The process in constructing the strategic plan is dependent upon the vision of the leader. The process in determining the vision is based on the specific goals that the leader is trying to accomplish within a defined period of time. The vision will dictate the long term goal of the organization. It is the blueprint and compass that will direct the action steps in the strategic plan.

The vision must be clear, concise and meet a broad objective that will have a systemic impact within the community. The vision is the passage way that allows stakeholders within the community to step into your mind and understand and interpret what your proposed strategic plan will accomplish.

The strategic plan is comprehensive and embodies the vision. The strategic plan breaks down your objectives, organizational structure, systematic plan, community impact and leadership within the organization. Your objective is your premeditated desired outcome from the prescribed plan.

Why is there a need for Community Engagement? When there exists a systemic issue that is detrimental to the growth of a community, a leader then crafts a strategic plan to fill the void within that set community.

As a leader one must understand that when organizing a community based project you must get the buy in from the residents of the community. The community is comprised of a body of people that reside in a particular geographical area and share common characteristics. The main component to any community engagement project is the people within that particular pre-determined area. The project must be arranged around a fixed time frame that will yield immediate and long term results.

The process of writing the strategic plan will yield two things; sustainable approaches and strategic partnerships so that the broader vision is accomplished. During the strategic plan there is a phase of community mapping to research the pockets and areas of most need. For example draw a map of your community and break it down into the following components:

- Businesses
- Residential homes
- Blighted areas
- Nuisance activity areas
- Green space
- Schools

This will give you a visual picture of the areas of most need within your community. The mapping process will assist with the planning phase with your community engagement project.

Through the research one will determine the following:

- What are the leading factors that caused the current issue within the community?

- What are some realistic solutions that can be implemented over a ten year time frame.
- What are the challenges and barriers that community organizers will face when implementing the community engagement project.

Various Types of Community Engagement

- Direct Service (People)
    - direct service involves physically being out into the streets of the community with organizing community blocks projects or by providing a
    - hands-on involvement to address immediate issues within the community
    - one-time projects or on-going projects at a set location or various locations within a set region that includes several communities
    - direct service immediate needs include services such as food, shelter, clothing or medical care

- Community Building
    - involves the re-development of a neighborhood. Revival of the sense of community with a series of stimulating activities which brings fills the gap and repairs the breach.

- Community Education
    - involves community residents, community school, agencies to address community concerns around the educational system in that school district.
    - community education is a platform for traditional and non-traditional teaching methods

used to promote learning, social development and assist students that are below average in their scholastic achievements.

- Economic Development
    - involves an action plan around the promotion of economic growth in a community. The improvement of the economic state of a community is dependent on fundamental building blocks; the educational system, the workforce, healthcare institutions
    - through direct service strategies are put into place to educate residents within the community around financial management
    - economic development also focuses on stabilizing the infrastructure of a city and state which will impact the smaller community that make up the city.

Target Audience

Determining your target audience is vital when creating your strategic plan. Organizations must have a specific target audience that will fit with the community engagement project. Can an organization have more than one target audience? Yes, but you must not lose sight of your vision. Unfortunately, some organizations try to facilitate multiple engagement projects within a community at one time without determining the target audience. When an organization takes on more than one project at a time it can lead to poor management and unclear results. Step #4 will go into detail about how to set up your "Time Line" for your projects. As you examine your target audience understand "the System" (framework) your organization must work within.

The System
- the framework to how your organization operates.

The Impact
- how many people do you want to serve through this community engagement project?

The Organization
- who are the key players that are facilitating the project?

The Shift
- what type of results do you want to see come from the project?

The Leadership
- what type of training program is in place to train residents within the community to continue with the project even after the community organization is complete?

Case Study (The History and Vision of Goodwill Industries International, Inc.)

"Goodwill was founded in 1902 in Boston by Rev. Edgar J. Helms, a Methodist minister and early social innovator. Helms collected used household goods and clothing in wealthier areas of the city, then trained and hired those who were poor to mend and repair the used goods. The goods were then resold or were given to the people who repaired them. The system worked, and the Goodwill philosophy of "a hand up, not a hand out" was born.

Dr. Helms' vision set an early course for what today has become a $4 billion nonprofit organization. Helms described Goodwill Industries as an "industrial program as well as a social service enterprise...a provider of employment, training and rehabilitation for people of limited employability, and a source of temporary assistance for individuals whose resources were depleted."

Times have changed, but Helms' vision remains constant: "We have courage and are unafraid. With the prayerful cooperation of millions of our bag contributors and of our workers, we will press on till the curse of poverty and exploitation is banished from mankind."

Vision
Goodwill works to enhance the dignity and quality of life of individuals and families by strengthening communities, eliminating barriers to opportunity, and helping people in need reach their full potential through learning and the power of work.

*Goodwills meet the needs of all job seekers, including programs for **youth**, **seniors**, **veterans**, and **people with disabilities**, **criminal backgrounds** and other specialized needs. Last year, Goodwill helped more than **9.8 million people** train for careers in industries such as banking, IT and health care, to name a few — and get the supporting services they needed to be successful — such as English language training, additional education, or access to transportation and child care.*

Write the Plan (The Concept)
Activity
1. Maintain a journal on your daily activities for the next 90 days to track your leadership habits.
2. Develop your strategic plan. Listed below are the components of a *"Strategic Plan"*.

- **Mission statement:** A description of your purpose. It answers the question of "Why does your organization exist?" What need does your organization fill?

- **Vision statement:** It is a short statement of the organization's future plans and offers a picture of what the organization will look like in five or more years.

- **SWOT (Strength, Weaknesses, Opportunities & Threats):** This is a very important step in your strategic planning. It is a summarized view of your current position, specifically your strengths, weaknesses, opportunities, and threats.

- **Competitive advantage:** Every organization needs to determine their competitive advantage. There is no need to duplicate a successfully run community engagement project that is already being implemented. In other words research and identify a need in the community and fill the void. Otherwise when your organization is compared to established community based projects it will prove to be very difficult to get funding and support.

- **Long-term strategic objectives:** Every organization should focus on strategic game plans that will build their organization in increments of 10 years. Organizations can break that down into short-term strategic focus areas in three-year time frames.

- **Strategies:** What is a *"Strategy"*? A strategy is a method in which you will execute your overall vision.

- **Short-term goals/priorities/initiatives:** When developing your strategic plan it is important to put your long-term objectives into short-term performance targets that will be accomplished within the first two years. Having small measurable goals will assist with you getting closer to your overall vision.

- **Action items/plans:** The daily operations of your organization are dependent upon your daily action steps. Typically your daily action steps are carried out by your teams within the organization. We will get into more details about how to develop teams in Step #5. Your daily action steps are what will keep the progress moving within your organization.

- **Organizational monitoring:** It is imperative that every organization maintains data on the work the organization is doing within the community. The data will reflect key performance indicators which will let you know if your work is on target with your monthly goals. We will discuss more about how to review the progress of your organization in Step #7.

- **Financial assessment:** To become self-sufficient it is imperative organizations keep good records to track their spending habits. This will help make future projection as well as identify areas in the budget to eliminate.

Strategic Plan at a Glance

Mission statement:

_____

Vision statement: _____

_____

SWOT: _____

_____

Competitive advantage: _____

_____

Long-term strategic objectives: _____

_____

Strategies: _____

_____

Short-term goals/priorities/initiatives: _____

_____

_____

Action items/plans: _____

_____

Organizational monitoring: _____

_____

Financial assessment: _____

_____

"Vision without action is daydream. Action without vision is nightmare."

~Japanese Proverb

STEP 2

CREATION OF TIMELINE

STEP 2

Creation of Timeline

Step 2: Creation of Timeline
The timeline is a significant tool in tracking and monitoring the forward movement of the organization. It will assist you in determining the cycles of your organization in ten year increments.

Timeline - *a graphic representation of the passage of time as a line. a linear representation of important events in the order in which they occurred.* **(Webster)**

Create Your Timeline

When was your organization incorporated?

_____

_____

When did your organization form your board of directors?

_____

_____

When did your organization receive its 501C3 status from the IRS?

_____

_____

What was the date of the launch event of your organization?

_____

_____

When did your organization receive the first grant?

_____

_____

When did your organization expand into its own facility?

_____

_____

When did your organization expand into multiple states?

_____

_____

These are just some questions to get you started into developing your timeline. Continue to add events that occurred within your organization by year, month and event.

REVIEW OF YOUR ORGANIZATION THE PAST 12 MONTHS

What goals have been accomplished? _____

_____

_____

_____

What are some of the barriers to the goals that you did not accomplish? _____

_____

_____

_____

TIMELINE MAPPING

Years 1-3, *Foundation Phase*

The foundation phase includes the following:

- Incorporation and formation of board of directions (determine your mission, vision and goals)
- Apply for 501C3 tax exempt status
- Organization the community engagement project (Launch Event)
- Creation of your organizations campaigns
- Applying for first grant opportunity
- Implement 1-2 programs within your designated community.

Years 4-6, *Stabilization Phase*

The stabilization phase includes the following:

- Acquired and maintained a multi-year grant opportunity with grant funders
- Gained a minimum of 3-5 corporate sponsors that contribute financially on a annual basis
- Clearly defined the organizations fixed budget (discussed in Step #3)
- Generated success stories from community engagement projects

Years 7-9, *Growth Phase*

The growth phase includes the following:

- Produce reports based on data gathered from years 1-9 of the number of people served in your target audience and community impact data based on community engagement projects
- Stable budget with fixed financial projections
- Stable board of directors, sub-committees and volunteers
- The alliance (network) is growing by 10% annually (discussed in Step #4)

Year 10, *Duplication Phase*, Step #8 will discuss in more detail.

The duplication phase includes the following:

- Assessment of the organization assets should be examined again in the ninth year
- Review growth strategies used in years 7-9
- Implement strategies for long term growth that can be reflected in ten year increments
- Discuss and review financial projections for the next ten years
- Research the industry and determine what will be trending in the next ten years around funding and resources needed to maintain the growth of the organization

Case Study (Goodwill Industries)

While Goodwill Industries has an amazing history and record of accomplishment, we cannot be satisfied while so many still need our services. Through the 21st Century Initiative, the organization seeks to improve the economic self-sufficiency of 20 million people and their families by 2020.

Again this case study speaks to strategic planning at its finest. It is important to plan five or more years out with specific goals. In Step #8 we will discuss establishing your organization for longevity.

<u>Creation of Timeline (Projection)</u>
Activity
Create your organization timeline map.
Example; Years 2015 -2025

Years 1-3:

_____

_____

_____

_____

_____

Years 4-6:

_____

_____

_____

_____

_____

Years 7-9:

_____

_____

_____

_____

_____

Year 10:

_____

_____

_____

_____

_____

Honesty and integrity are by far the most important assets of an entrepreneur.

~Zig Ziglar

STEP 3

EXAMINE YOUR ASSETS

STEP 3
Examine Your Assets

Step 3: Examine your assets
Whether your organization is newly established or has been operating over 10 years the strength of the organization relies on the assets. Determining the assets of a organization should be done over a dedicated period of 30 days.

Your assets are not just a culmination of liquid cash in your organization bank account or property. It is the total sum of what is in your "NETWORK". In this step you will determine what you already have acquired and in Step #3 we will discuss how to build and expand your assets through your network.

Unfortunately, many organizations don't realize that a large percentage of your assets are your board members, sub-committee members, volunteers, business and civic partnerships and the people that you serve (target audience).

A organization assets are divided into the following categories:
1. Liquid cash in the bank
    - How much cash can the organization touch that is not connected to a loan?
2. Property (owned)
    - Does the organization own the title of the property? The value of that property equates to a dollar amount that will go into the overall acquired assets of the organization.

3. The Network (agencies, institutions, board members, committee members, business and civic leaders and people of the community)
   - The people within your organization have a value and most organizations don't calculate that into the equation.
   - How do you determine the value of the "the Network"?
       - Calculate what each person or entity in your network brings to your organization. Do they bring resources that help push the vision forward or are they a liability that detracts the value of the vision and stagnates it progress?

As you are determining the assets of the organization you will want to pull in your board of directors to assist with the process.

You can divide your board into three teams:
1. Network Assets
   a. What are the assets in the NETWORK? This team will evaluate the total sum of what the organization has within the alliance.
2. Liquid, Earned Income, On-going Assets
   a. *Example:* Goodwill Industries acquires their earned assets from the retail business which yields on-going income into the organization. This team will evaluate the earned income business model of your organization. What's bringing in the *MONEY*?

3. Expense Review

30 Day Asset Determination Period (New & Established Organizations)

Day 1 – Day 15

Construct an inventory of your organizations assets by examining the following key areas:

1. Board of Directors (40%)
2. Sub Committees (15%)
3. Volunteer Database (10%)
4. Business Collaborations (15%)
5. Civic Partnerships (10%)
6. People Served to Date (Target Audience) (10%)

Your board of directors should focus on marketing the organization and creating a funding plan that reflects a ten year financial plan. Your sub-committees support the strategic plan of the board of directors and they become ambassadors in the community assisting with the execution of the daily actions steps. Your volunteers are the heart beat of your organization because they contribute their skill set in various areas of your organization to strengthen the foundation. Your business collaborations and civic partnerships are vital because they are extensions from your organization into their network. Strategic partnerships can grow your organizations assets by 10% annually.

This process is it critical to determine if the people in your network are adding value to your vision.

See diagram A: Assets

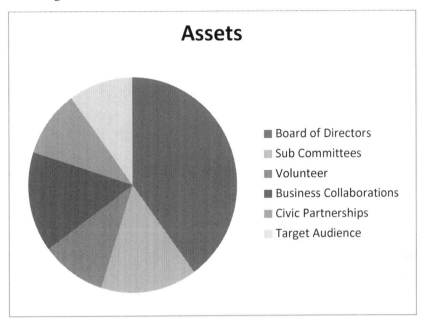

Assets

- Board of Directors
- Sub Committees
- Volunteer
- Business Collaborations
- Civic Partnerships
- Target Audience

Day 16 – Day 25

Construct an inventory of your organizations assets (income / property) by examining the following key areas:

1. Liquid cash in organization bank account as of today.
   $_____

2. List the annual grants that your organization receives.
   _____
   _____

3. List your corporate sponsors.
   _____
   _____

4. Profits (Earned Income) On-Going Income for Organization
    - What is your service/product?

      _____

      _____

      _____

    - Does your product reach a broader population?

      _____

      _____

      _____

    - Does your organization own *"Intellectual Property"*? Example; training workbooks, books, etc.

      _____

      _____

      _____

Day 26 – Day 30

Construct an inventory of your organizations **expenses** by examining the following key areas:

1. Fixed Expense (Examples)
    - Rent
    - Insurance
2. Variable Expense (Examples)
    - Project expenses
    - Contractual stipend agreements

Fixed Expense (List your fixed expenses)
    - _____
    - _____

- _____
- _____
- _____

Variable Expense (List your variable expenses)

- _____
- _____
- _____
- _____
- _____

Case Study (Goodwill Revenue Sources)

Data As of 2013

- **Retail sales:** $3.79 billion (Earned Income)
- **Industrial and service contract work:** $647 million
- **Government grants:** $90 million
- **Corporate and foundation grants:** $27 million
- **Individual gifts/Endowments/Fees for services:** $46 million
- **Government support for mission services:** $455 million

As previously noted, Goodwill's major source of funds come from "Earned Income" through their retail sales. This provides a model on how to generate on-going assets in a philanthropic industry.

Examine Your Assets (The Value)
Activity
Write down some "Key Assets" that your organization currently has acquired.

_____

_____

_____

_____

_____

Create and or update your list of contacts in excel. Includes all contact information on contacts within your network. This document can be used to upload for social media campaigns.

"*There are two primary choices in life: to accept conditions as they exist, or accept the responsibility for changing them.*"

~Denis Waitley

STEP 4

DEVELOP A
STRATEGIC
ALLIANCE
(THE NETWORK)

STEP 4

Develop a Strategic Alliance
(the NETWORK)

Step 4: Develop a strategic alliance (the NETWORK)

The strategic alliance (the NETWORK) is the third building step in the process of community engagement. On an annual basis it is good to grow your network by a minimum of 10%.

If in 2014 you have a network size of 100 people in 2015 you should at the very minimum grow to 110 people within your network.

Alliance - *a union or association formed for mutual benefit, especially between countries or organizations.* **(Webster)**

Network - *a group or system of interconnected people or things.* **(Webster)**

The strategy for growing your network should reflect a system that the board of directors have in place.

When developing your alliance it is important to have a clear understand of your vision and to know the needs of the organization. Step #1 should have allowed you to clearly identify the need and the vision of the organization. Through that process you have discovered the resources needed to accomplish the vision.

Now, it is time to examine who you already have in the network and members you need to enroll to successfully see the project implemented with desired results.

Who do your currently have in your alliance? _____

_____

Your alliance should reflect a picture of where you want to see your organization in the next 10 years. Don't just select people to be a part of your alliance because they are just excited about your vision.

What skill set or resources do they bring to the table?

_____

_____

_____

Once you have determined who you currently have within your alliance then you can begin to fill in the gaps with specific people that you will need.

An effective strategic alliance should encompass a *Community Marketing Engagement Plan* which allows for *Cross Marketing* among alliance members. Community marketing engagement involves two or more organizations collaborating on marketing strategies that will broaden the base of both organizations.

Strategic Alliance (the NETWORK) Pillars
- Marketing
  - Brand Awareness
- Revenue
  - Grant Opportunities
  - Corporate Sponsors
  - Earned Income
- Shared Network
- In-Kind Contributions

See Diagram B: Strategic Alliance (the NETWORK)

Diagram B

An evenly proportioned matrix of what makes up your alliance will bear significant weight to the projection of desired results.

Develop a strategic alliance (the NETWORK Diagram)
As we develop the network examine the past 12 months and the value that each essential member has brought to the network.

LIST THE TOP 10 ALLIANCE MEMBERS

1. _____

2. _____

3. _____

4. _____

5. _____

6. _____

7. _____

8. _____

9. _____

10. _____

DESCRIBE WHAT EACH ALLIANCE MEMBER HAS BROUGHT OF VALUE TO THE NETWORK

1. _____
2. _____
3. _____
4. _____
5. _____
6. _____
7. _____
8. _____
9. _____
10. _____

Case Study (Goodwill Industries International, Inc.)

Goodwill's network of 165 independent, community-based Goodwill's in the United States and Canada offers customized training and services for individuals who want to find a job, pursue a credential or degree, and strengthen their finances. Each local Goodwill must be accredited, apply for membership and meet certain criteria established by Goodwill Industries International (GII).

Goodwill Industries established an internationally recognized brand which increased the organizations assets. The trademark process is vital to the expansion of any organization. Why should your organization want a trademark? It will not only further legitimize your organization but it will help with the branding expansion and organization recognition. Example, most toddlers can't read but they know McDonald's when they see the golden arches.

The strategic alliance (the NETWORK) should also have a technology component that enables the members within the network to share resources.

Activity
Create a diagram (web) and chart the type of people, agencies, civic organizations and businesses that you need to develop into your network over the next ten years.

See Diagram C: Strategic Alliance (the NETWORK)

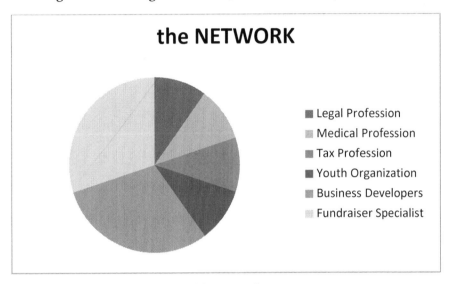

Diagram C

"It is hard to fail, but it is worse never to have tried to succeed."

~Theodore Roosevelt

STEP 5

DEVELOP TEAMS

STEP 5
Develop Teams

Step 5: Develop Teams
The teams you establish will comprise the structure of your organization and we have all heard the old adage "You are only strong as your weakest link." Well, in the community engagement arena you are only effective as your weakest team. Step #5 takes us through the process of determining the leadership traits and abilities within your teams.

According to "A Tool to Develop Collective Leadership for Community Change" the concept of collective leadership

> *is a way for diverse groups of people in our communities to hold purpose, direction, and action cooperatively. (Center for Ethical Leadership) Collective leadership requires us to expand our notion of leadership from the solo perspective of "I" to include the powerful "We"- keeping both the "I" and the "We" as equal partners. Collective leadership invites power to be shared and finds the way for all of us to contribute our gifts- whatever our formal positions. It has a fluid quality that allows people to take risks and be part of what has meaning for them.*

In developing teams your *Project Manager* plays a vital role in establishing and coordinating the team structure. The project manager should be skilled in organizational development.

This person will:
- Schedule and facilitate team meetings
- Maintain records on meeting notes for reference
- Identify resources needed to complete the project

- Determine strengths and weaknesses among the team members
- Create actions plans and set reasonable dates for completion of the project

To begin the process of developing active teams within your organization:

1. Analyze and write down what type of teams you will need to fulfill your community engagement project.

_____

_____

_____

_____

_____

2. Meeting of the minds
- Schedule a date when the team will come together in one place to meet.

- Projected Date: _____

3. Start the dialogue
- Have a list of pre-set topics to discuss to keep the group on track throughout the meeting.

Topic #1 _____

Topic #2 _____

Topic #3 _____

4. Analyze strengths and weaknesses within the teams.

   Questions?
   - What strengths does everyone bring to the
     organization?

     _____
     _____
     _____
     _____
     _____
     _____
     _____
     _____

     If the teams have been in operation of more than
     12 months examine what has worked well over
     the past 12 months?

     _____
     _____
     _____
     _____

   - What weaknesses currently exist within the
     group? If the teams have been in operation of
     more than 12 months examine what needs
     improvement or change?

     _____
     _____

_____

_____

- What opportunities are around us? If the teams have been in operation of more than 12 months examine what opportunities operating consistently to achieve the vision of the community engagement project?

_____

_____

_____

_____

- What obstacles (barriers) does your team foresee as the project is being implemented? If the teams have been in operation of more than 12 months examine what obstacles the team faced in the implementation of the project.

_____

_____

_____

_____

5. Organize teams based on a blended approach.
   - After discovering the strengths and weaknesses within the larger group, then proceed to create break out groups of fewer people that will take on various roles within the community engagement project.

- Have a balanced group that will evenly represent various phases of the project.

- BREAK OUT GROUP #1

  _____

- BREAK OUT GROUP #2

  _____

- BREAK OUT GROUP #3

  _____

- BREAK OUT GROUP #4

  _____

6. Set deliverable deadline dates. (In Step #2 we discussed the Creation of the Timeline) It is very important to have a set time dedicated to the completion of the project.

Develop Teams (Formation)
Activity
Team Building Exercise

1. What type of teams do you need?

   _____
   _____

_____
_____
_____

2. Schedule a date for your first team meeting.

_____

3. The Dialogue
   a. Schedule for a minimum of a two-hour meet up.

4. Determining your team assets
   a. Strengths:

   _____
   _____
   _____
   _____

   b. Weaknesses:

   _____
   _____
   _____
   _____

   c. Opportunities:

   _____
   _____
   _____
   _____

   d. Threats:

   _____

_____

_____

_____

5. Project deadline dates.

    a. Phase 1 Project Description: _____

        _____

        _____

        • Project Deadline Date: _____

    b. Phase 2 Project Description: _____

        _____

        _____

        • Project Deadline Date: _____

    c. Phase 3 Project Description: _____

        _____

        _____

        • Project Deadline Date: _____

    d. Phase 4 Project Description: _____

        _____

        _____

The dialogue among leaders within the team is what breathes life to the coordination of the project. It allows for interaction among leaders, civic organizations and community members.

According to the *Center for Ethical Leadership "Collective Leadership"* is described as *"listening to those who want to contribute ideas and valuing their perspective."*

Team Assets (In Step #2 we learned the approach on how to identify our organizational assets.)

Successful organizing is based on the recognition that people get organized because they, too, have a vision.

~Paul Wellstone

STEP 6

IMPLEMENTATION (EXECUTE)

STEP 6
Implementation (Execute)

Step 6: Implementation (Execute)
Step six is where it all counts! The first five steps were preparing you for the execution of your strategic plan. Step #6 is about the execution of the project that you envision to be displayed within your community.

Implementation - *the process of putting a decision or plan into effect; execution.* **(Webster)**

The implementation step is vital to the fulfillment of the vision. If the strategic plan is never put into action then the time invested in creating the strategic plan bears NO VALUE. The hours invested into the development of the "Strategic Plan" then become a "depreciating asset."

The execution of a project can be broken down into the following phases:

1. Establish the start date of the project
   - Start Date _____

2. Establish the completion date of the project
   - Completion Date _____

3. Use the breakdown of the 4 phases of the project from Step #5
   - Phase #1
   - Phase #2
   - Phase #3
   - Phase #4

Project Management - *is the process and activity of planning, organizing, motivating, and controlling resources, procedures and protocols to achieve specific goals in scientific or daily problems.* **(Webster)**

From Step #5 your organization would have determined the lead *project manager* for the community engagement project based on the SWOT analysis.

List Project Manager: _____

What are you *"Desired Outcomes"* from the community engagement project?

_____
_____
_____
_____
_____
_____
_____
_____
_____

<u>Implementation (The execution of your strategy.)</u>
Activity

1, 2, 3 GET SET....GO!!!

Now is the time to execute the first 12 months of your strategic plan.

"The journey of a thousand miles begins with one step."

~Lao Tzu

STEP 7

Review & Edit

STEP 7
Review & Edit

Step 7: Review & Edit
In order to maintain the effectiveness and the longevity of any organization it is essential to review the successes and challenges. A great way to assist organizations during the *"Review & Edit"* period is to have tracked the following in an *"Organizational Development Log Book"*:

1. Daily action steps
2. Monthly goals met
3. Quarterly goals met
4. Obstacles and barriers in achieving your goals
5. New partners acquired
6. New funding sources

List your short-term successes from phase 1 of your project.

_____

_____

_____

_____

List some of the challenges that you faced during the first 6 months of your project.

_____

_____

_____

_____

Review & Edit (Maintenance)
Activity

After the first six months of implementing these steps it is time to review your progress. Perhaps some adjustments may be required for forward movement.

List adjustments that need to be made with the strategic plan.

_____

_____

_____

_____

TIPS FOR HOW TO MAINTANE THE GROWTH OF YOUR ORGANIZATION!

1. Review organizational goals associated with the overall vision.

2. Review organizational results with from data collection.

3. Did you meet the goal from the community engagement project?

4. Review of internal and external organizational structure.

5. Does the alliance (the network) contribute to progression of the overall vision?

6. Review board of directors management and contributions to the overall vision.

7. Identify new measureable goals that will aid in the forward movement of the overall vision.

8. Identify standards for evaluating your organization to include the following:
   - below expectations
   - meets expectations
   - exceeds expectations

9. Create a performance plan to include desired results, measureable goals and standards for success.

10. Get feedback about your organization performance with each community engagement project from your target audience. This will ensure that the project being implemented is relevant and beneficial to the intended community.

"*We are what we repeatedly do. Excellence, therefore, is not an act but a habit.*"

~Aristotle

STEP 8

THE RIPPLE EFFECT

STEP 8
The Ripple Effect

Step 8: The Ripple Effect

Ten years from now where do you want to see your organization? How many people will your organization have served? What will the data show on your programs effectiveness?

The effectiveness of any organization will be determined if the organization can arrive to a place of stability and duplicate its efforts decade to decade. Organizations that maintain to the tenth year should have a clearly defined brand and message that the community has adopted. It is the people from the community that will carry the name of the organization on for future generations.

It is very important that during the first 10 years of the organization to build trust with the community your organization serves. The management team of the organization should possess integrity and focus on action steps that will support the broader vision of the organization.

The organization should multiply in the following areas:

- Volunteers
- Corporate Sponsors
- Residents from the community that bought into the vision

Will your organization become a household name? What type of impact and impression will you leave on the minds and hearts of the people your organization serves?

By the tenth year the organization should be self-sustaining from earned income based on the information we covered in Step #3.

A *Ripple* is often presented with a visual depiction of water by being *a small wave or series of waves on the surface of water, especially as caused by an object dropping into it or a slight breeze.*

Effect - *a change that is a result or consequence of an action or other cause.* **(Webster)**

The Ripple Effect (10 Year Plan)
Activity

Write a five page description on your organization 10 years out from now. Describe the accomplishments, the clients you served and projects completed. Start the outline of your "Ripple Effect" description in the space below.

_____

_____

_____

_____

_____

_____

_____

_____

_____

_____

_____

_____

_____

_____

_____

_____

_____

_____

_____

<u>Case Study</u>
Based on a case study "The School's Role in Developing Civic
Engagement: A Study of Adolescents in Twenty-Eight
Countries"

> *"Schools achieve the best results in fostering civic*
> *engagement when they rigorously teach civic content and skills,*
> *ensure an open classroom climate for discussing issues, emphasize*
> *the importance of the electoral process, and encourage a*
> *participative school culture."*

One would have to concede that the educational system is a
vital component into the dynamics of community
development. The cited phrase above supports the assertion
that priming the minds of our youth while in school will
create the appetite for community engagement.

"In order to succeed, your desire for success should be greater than your fear of failure."

~Bill Cosby

VIEW ON COMMUNITY ENGAGEMENT

TODAY IS THE DAY TO MAKE CHANGE WITHIN YOUR COMMUNITY!

I want to inspire the reader to go beyond the normal traditions of community engagement. Open your eyes and chart a new course for engaging community members.

Never allow the lack of assets stop you from getting started or expanding your organization. Think of strategies to create *earned income* for your organization and **EXECUTE** on those strategies.

Think outside the box and create!

Remember, find a need in the marketplace and fill the void.

Your creative ideas are still yet to be released. Yes, this is the time to **EXECUTE**. Follow the steps and you will build a stable system that will duplicate decade to decade.

~Catherine Trotter

"A goal is a dream with a deadline."

~Napoleon Hill

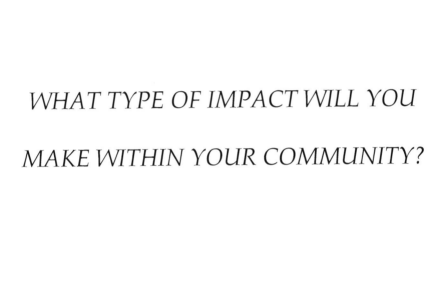

WHAT TYPE OF IMPACT WILL YOU

MAKE WITHIN YOUR COMMUNITY?

ARE YOU READY TO BUILD THE

"SYSTEM" FOR YOUR

ORGANIZATION?

CASE STUDIES

Building Community Capacity "A Definitional Framework
and Case Studies from a Comprehensive Community
Inititative
Robert J. Chaskin
University of Chicago, Urban Affairs
Vol. 36 No. 2001

A Review of Collaborative Partnerships as a Strategy for
Improving Community Health
Stergios Tsai Roussos and Stephen B. Fawcett,
Review of Public Health
Vol. 21 May 2000

The School's Role in Developing Civic Engagement: A
Study of Adolescents in Twenty-Eight Countries
Judith Torney-Purta
Applied Developmental Science
Vol. 6, Issue 4, 2002

A Tool to Develop Collective Leadership for Community
Change
Patricia Hughes with contributions by: Nienow, Ruder, Hale
and Rollins
Center for Ethical Leadership
2005

"Knowing is not enough; we must apply.
Willing is not enough; we must do."

~Johann Wolfgang von Goethe

ABOUT THE AUTHOR

Catherine Trotter was born and raised in Prince George's County Maryland, educated in the public school system and graduated from Northwestern High School. Ms. Trotter received formal training from Morgan State University located in Baltimore Maryland, where she earned a B.S. in Political Science in 2002. Catherine has 12 years of experience as a Project Manager. In 2002 Ms. Trotter established *House of New Beginnings, Inc.* a 501C3 non-profit organization and has since expanded the program to *New Beginnings Youth Development & Coaching Program*. In that program she provides professional development training workshops to youth and young adults. In 2005, Ms. Trotter launched her consulting business *Project Management Services* providing business consulting services for growing companies. Then in 2014 Ms. Trotter established the *Speak Life Tour* giving a platform for youth in the community to perform and showcase their talents in the area of performing and visual arts.

Ms. Trotter has been speaking publicly for 12 years at schools, community and business events and churches. She has consulted with several organizations under the umbrella of project management around strategic planning. Ms. Trotter has acquired experience in organizing community based programs and building networks between civic organizations, community residents, businesses, schools and churches. She is focused on assisting businesses both non-profit and for-profit to achieve their goals through strategic planning.

During Ms. Trotter's professional career she has consulted with state and federally funded civic organizations throughout the state of Maryland. She has also consulted with for-profit businesses in developing new business and marketing strategies. Her expertise and knowledge has proven results with various business entities, including: BBE Contractors, LLC, Moral Treasures, LLC, Women's Challenge, Inc., CLASSY 5, Trustworthy Staffing Solutions, Baltimore Citizens for Positive Change and Our Vision, Inc.

The collective body within a community can transform and reshape itself to yield resources for the community.

~Catherine Trotter

The 7 Habits of Highly Effective People

Habit #2 "Begin with the end in mind"

~Stephen Covey

"Leadership is not about titles, positions or flowcharts. It is about one life influencing another."

~ John C. Maxwell

CONTACT INFORMATION

Catherine Trotter
PO Box 7107
Baltimore MD 21218

Toll Free: 1.888.410.8430
Office: 202.827.7448

Email: **ct@catherinetrotter.com**
Website: **www.catherinetrotter.com**

Made in the USA
San Bernardino, CA
16 February 2016